Yoffe.Studio

MW01118799

HOW TO DRAW CUTE THINGS

100+

DRAWINGS
OF EVERYTHING

step-by-step
tutorial for kids

CONTENTS

HOW TO USE THIS BOOK

PREPARE YOUR DRAWING SUPPLIES

Sharp pencil & eraser

Before you begin, prepare your favorite drawing tools. Make sure you have an eraser and a well-sharpened pencil in your set.

Colored pencils & bonus materials

We believe that colored pencils are the best option for coloring. However, you may use colored markers if you wish. Use QR code to download a free bonus materials with coloring examples.

FOLLOW THE STEP-BY-STEP INSTRUCTIONS

①

Guidelines

Start your drawing by adding a guidelines and simple shapes. Make thin lines without pressing hard on the pencil.

②

Sketch

Stick to simple shapes to sketch the body or head, then add other elements step-by-step. Use gentle lines. In case you make a mistake, you can quickly and easily correct it with an eraser.

③

Outline

Once the sketch is ready, you can outline it. Here you can make bold lines by using a soft pancil or marker. After finish you can areate thin guidelines for the shadows to make your drawing more realistic.

④

Color

The last step is coloring. You can use colored pencils or markers. Be careful with the shadow areas if you decide to use markers. Color the light areas first, then the dark ones.

BUNNY

PRACTICE

FOX

PRACTICE

KITTEN

PRACTICE

MOUSE

PRACTICE

PANDA

PRACTICE

PIG

PRACTICE

HIPPO

PRACTICE

PENGUIN

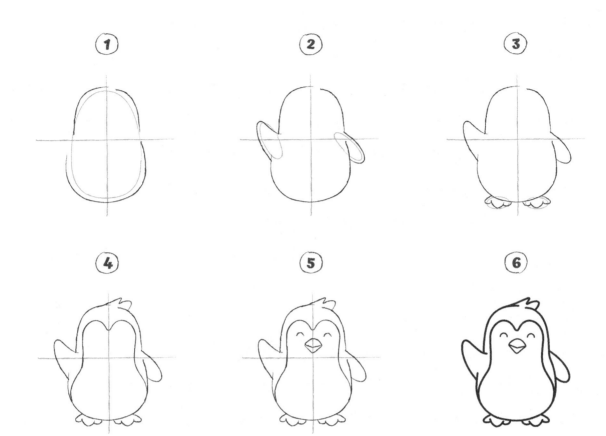

PRACTICE

PUPPY

PRACTICE

SQUIRREL

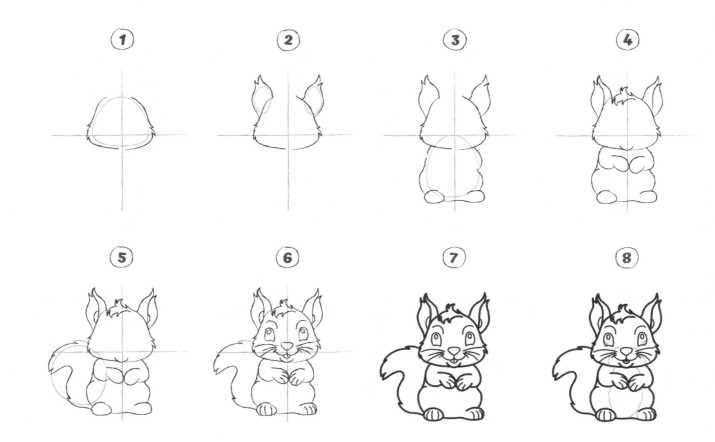

① ② ③ ④

⑤ ⑥ ⑦ ⑧

PRACTICE

CACTUS

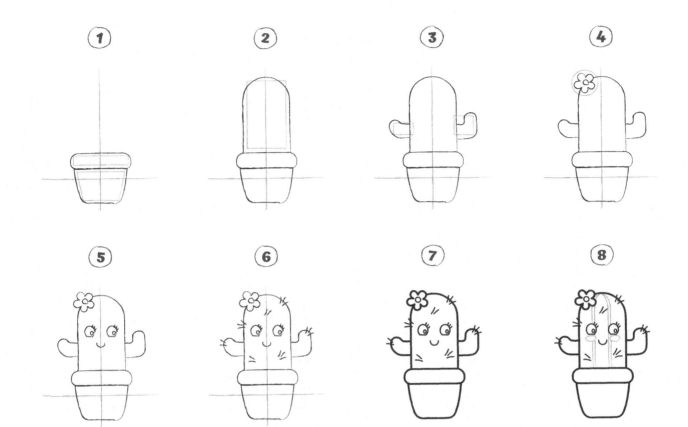

PRACTICE

CATERPILLAR

PRACTICE

SUNFLOWER

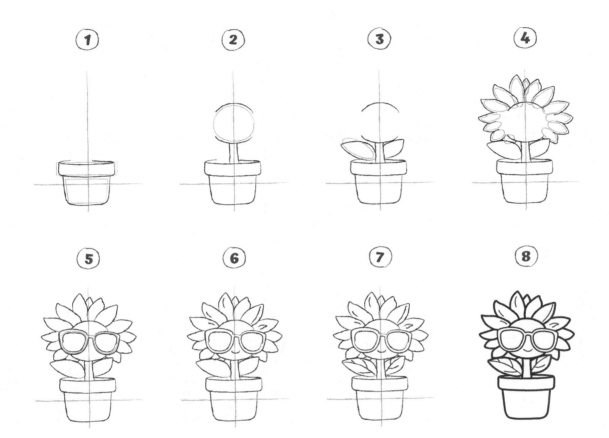

PRACTICE

HONEY BEE

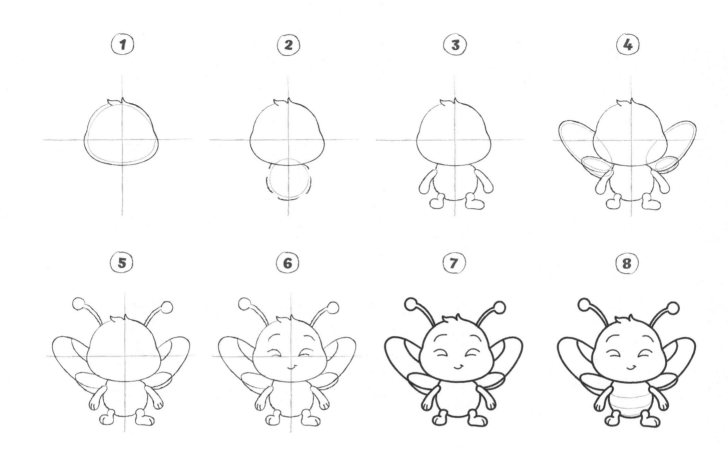

PRACTICE

MASHROOM

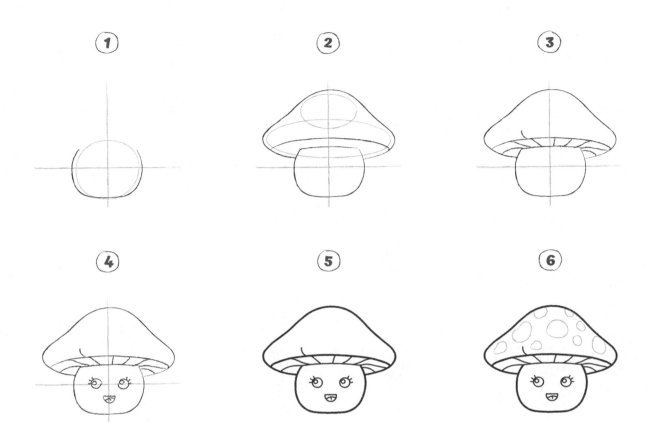

① ② ③

④ ⑤ ⑥

PRACTICE

GRASSHOPPER

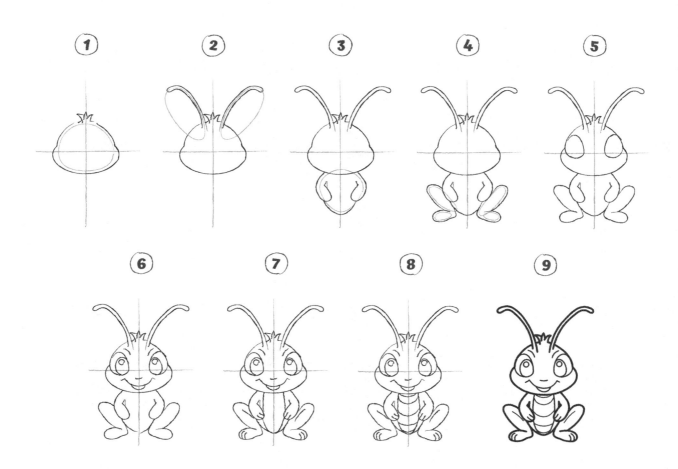

PRACTICE

ALOE

PRACTICE

ANT

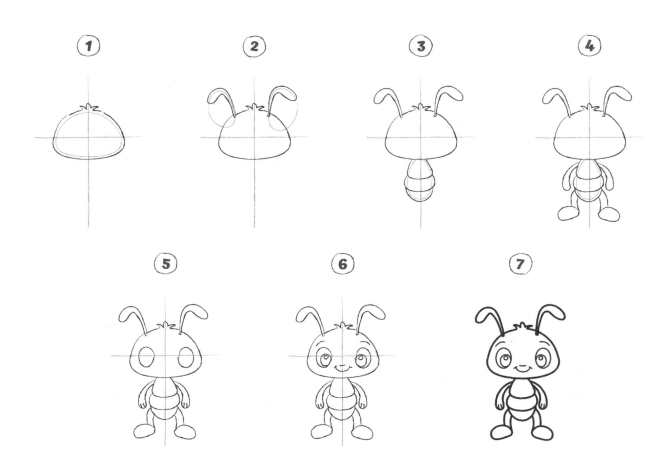

PRACTICE

LADYBUG

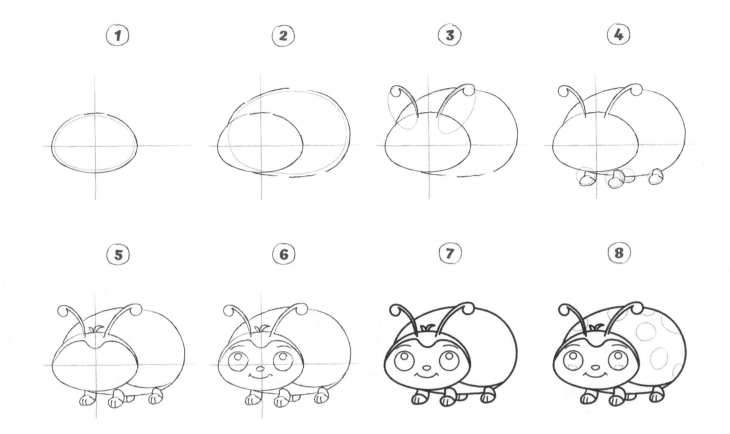

PRACTICE

BAMBOO

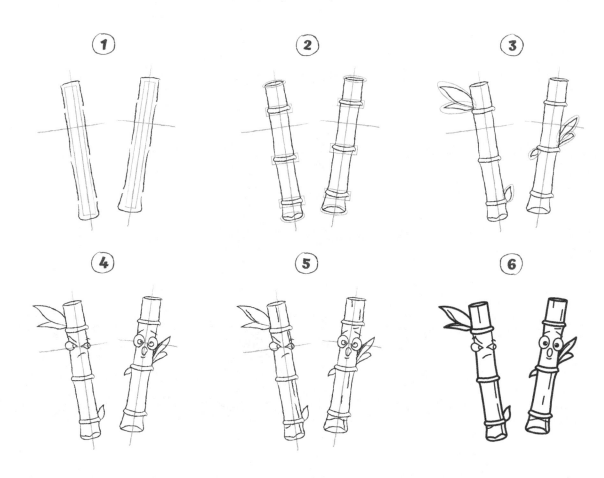

①　②　③

④　⑤　⑥

PRACTICE

SUN & CLOUD

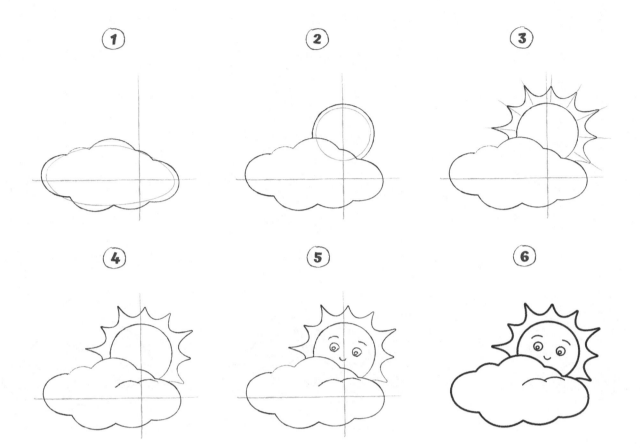

PRACTICE

RAINBOW

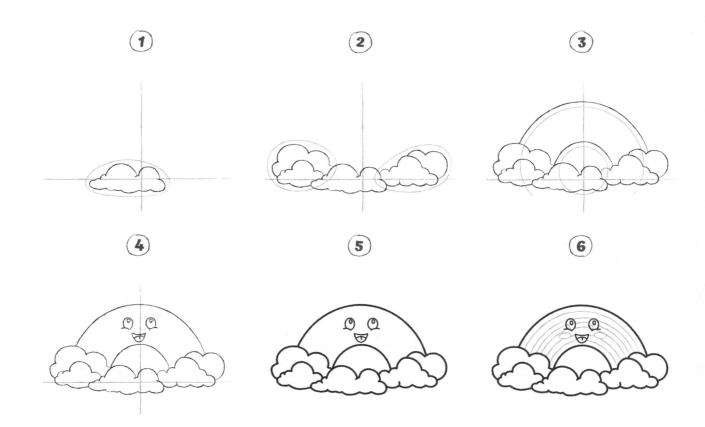

PRACTICE

MOON & STAR

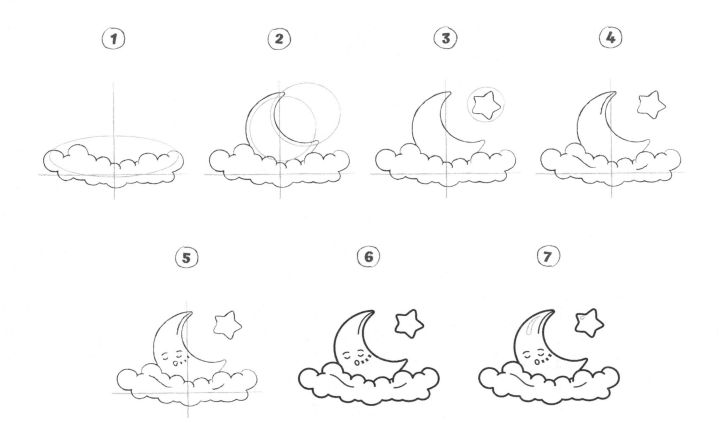

PRACTICE

UMBRELLA

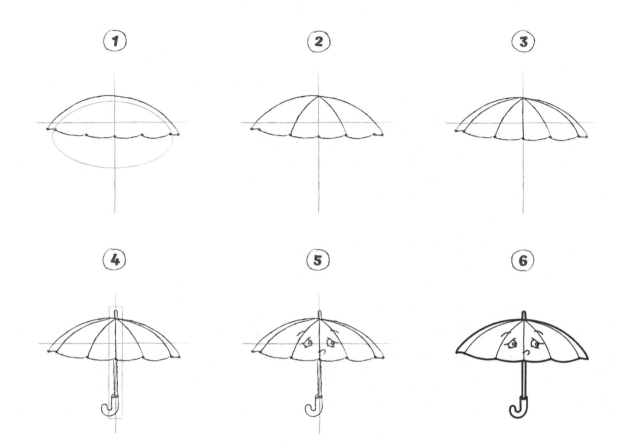

PRACTICE

WIND & THUNDERCLOUD

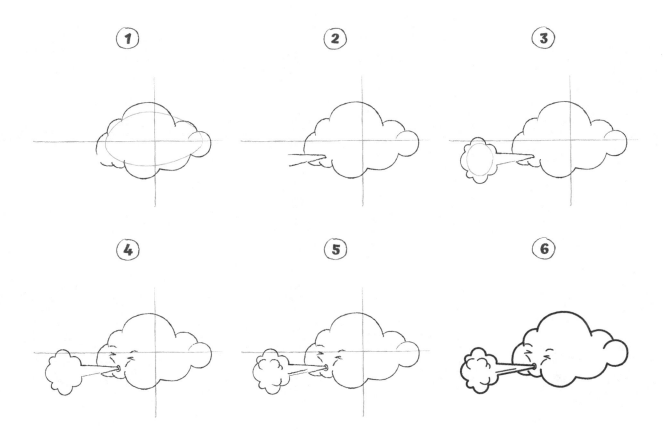

PRACTICE

TORNADO

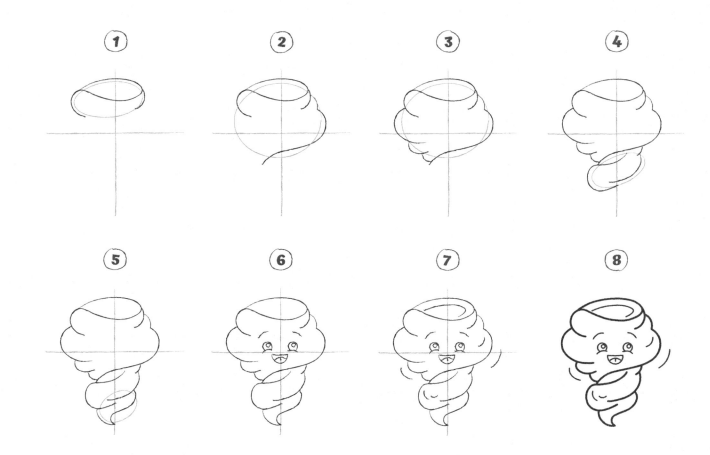

PRACTICE

THERMOMETER

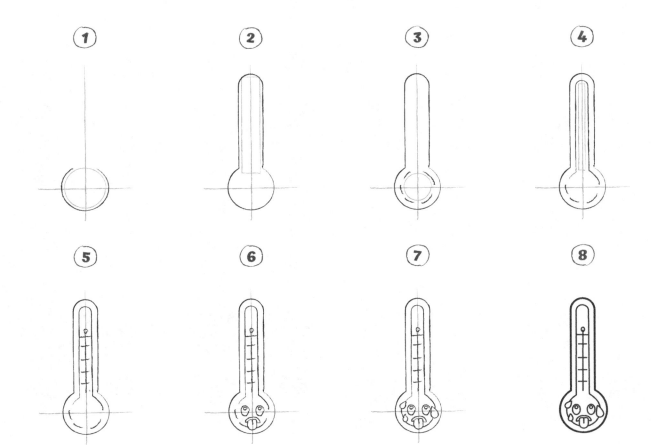

PRACTICE

SNOWFLAKE

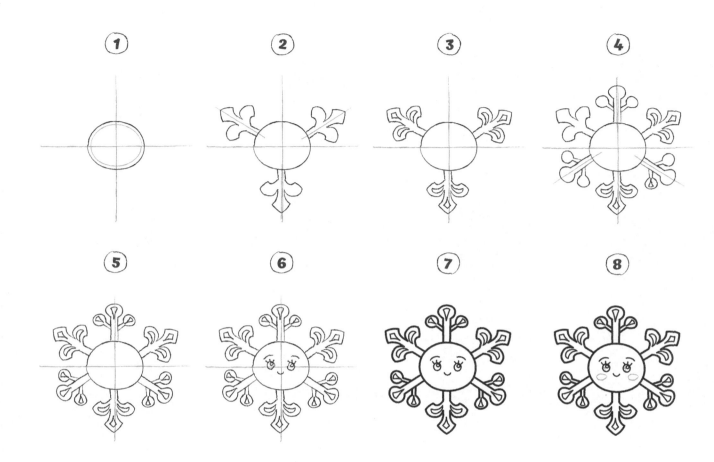

① ② ③ ④

⑤ ⑥ ⑦ ⑧

PRACTICE

LIGHTNING

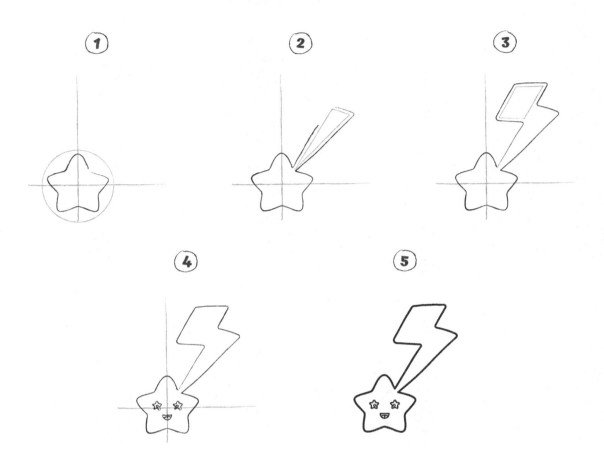

PRACTICE

RAINDROP

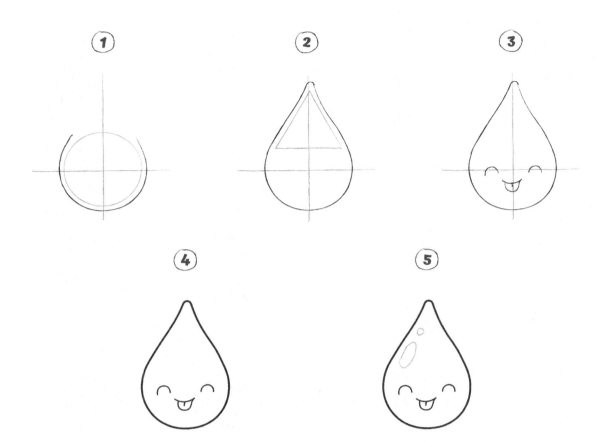

PRACTICE

CUP OF COFFE

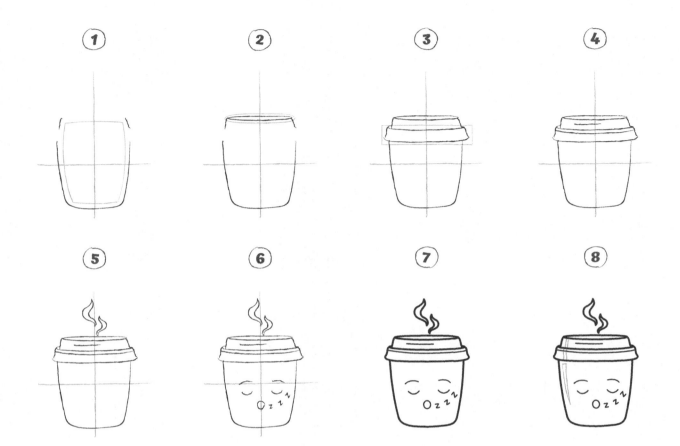

PRACTICE

BOTTLE OF MILK

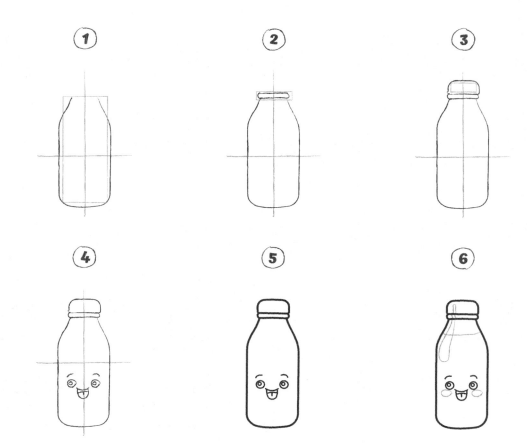

PRACTICE

PIECE OF BREAD

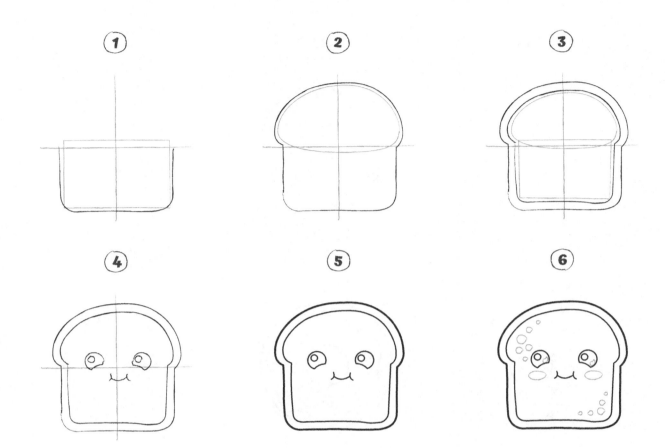

PRACTICE

DONUT

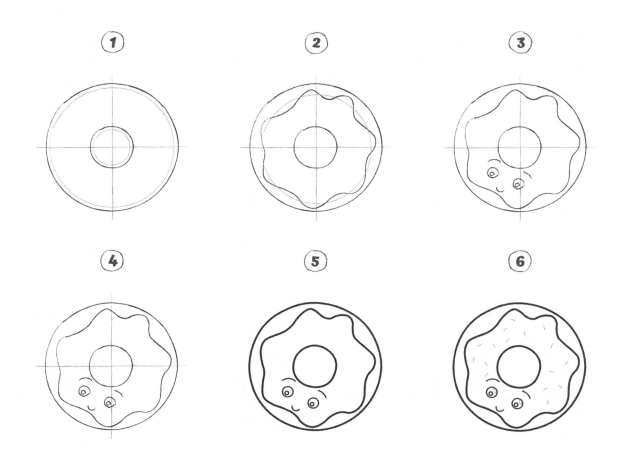

PRACTICE

FRIED EGGS

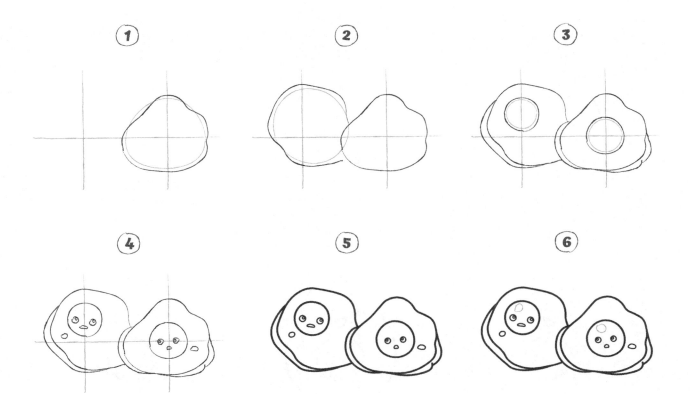

PRACTICE

AVOCADO

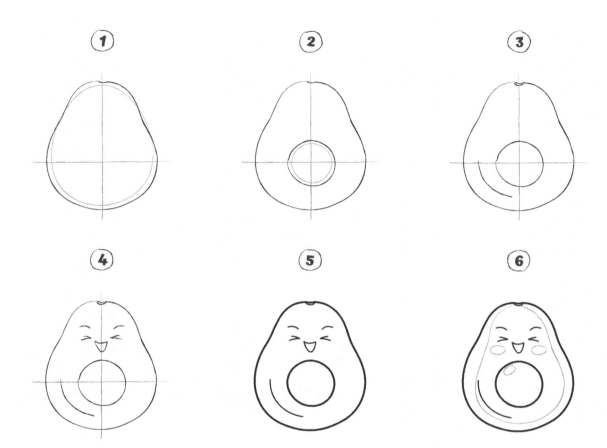

PRACTICE

ICE CREAM

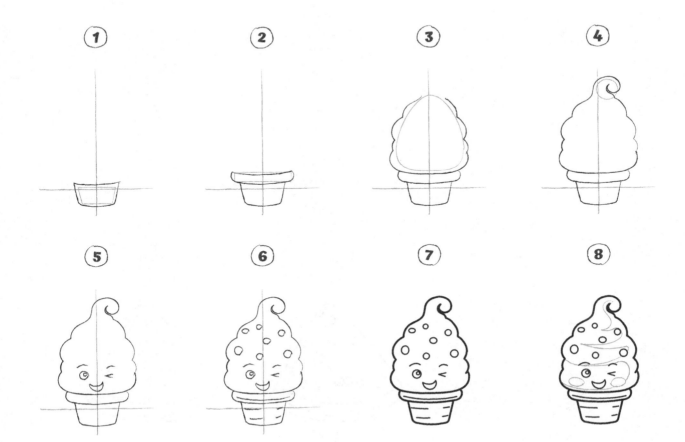

PRACTICE

WATERMELON

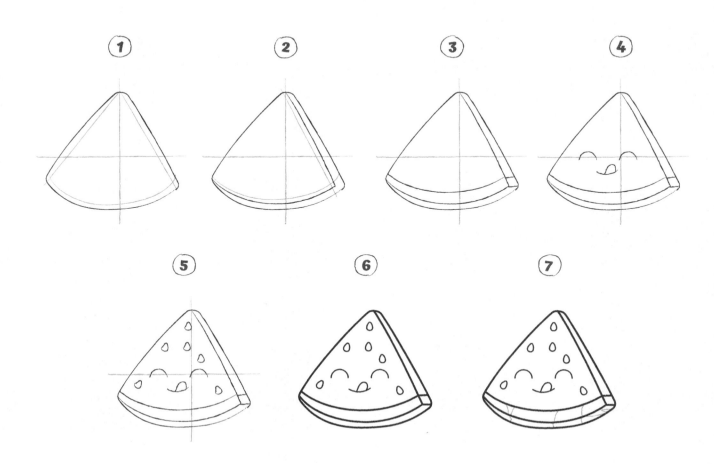

PRACTICE

STRAWBERRY

PRACTICE

BROCCOLI

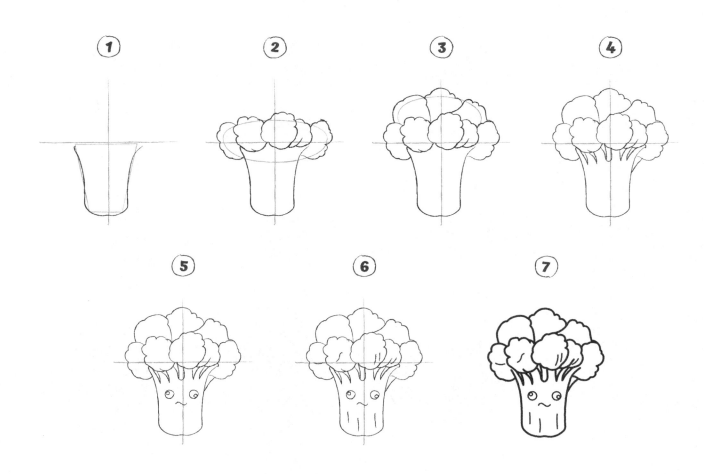

PRACTICE

PUMPKIN

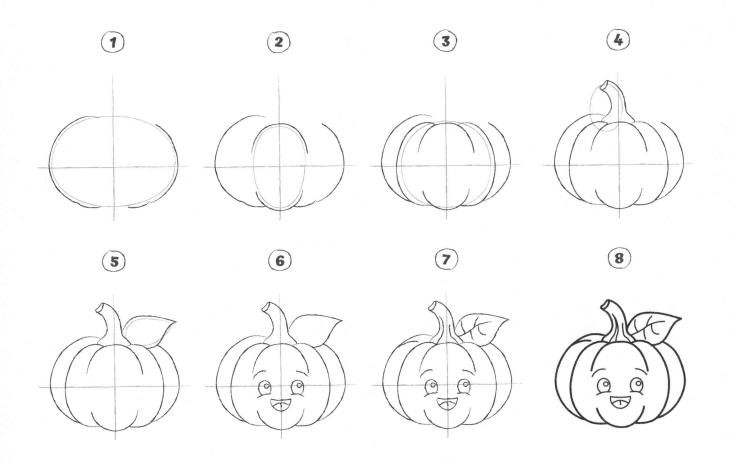

PRACTICE

LEMON

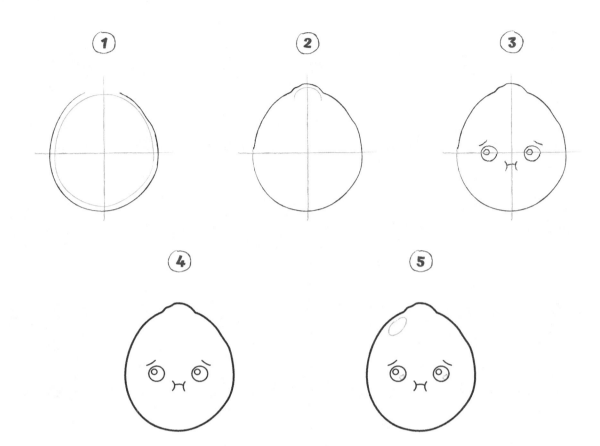

PRACTICE

FORK & SPOON

PRACTICE

PLATE

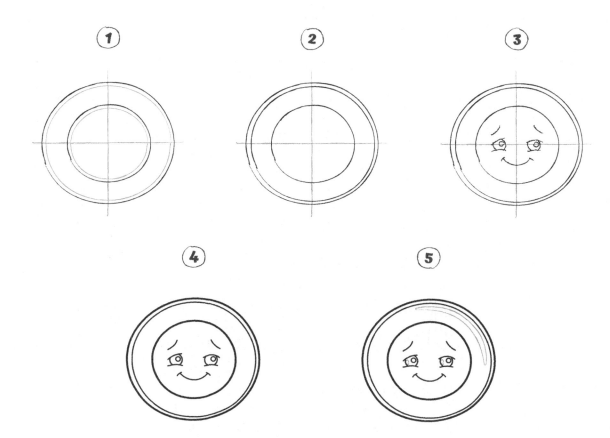

① ② ③

④ ⑤

PRACTICE

MUG

PRACTICE

GLASS OF JUICE

PRACTICE

SOUP POT

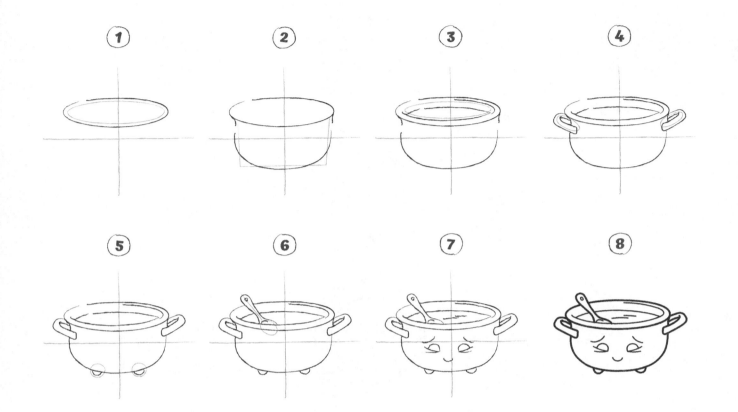

PRACTICE

FRYING PAN

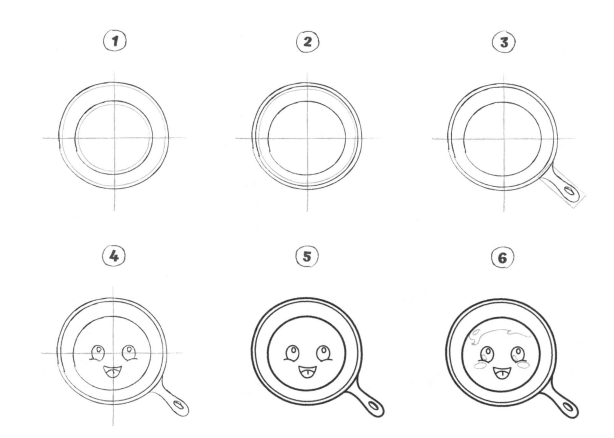

PRACTICE

LADLE

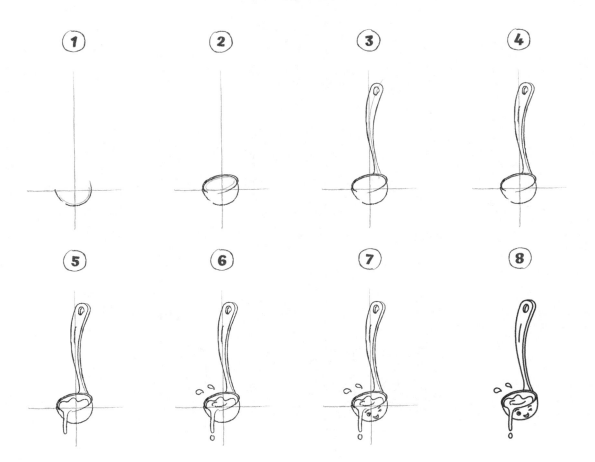

PRACTICE

CUTTING BOARD

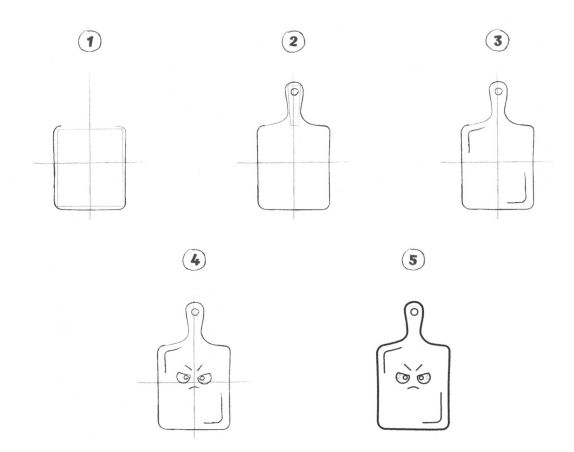

PRACTICE

GRATER

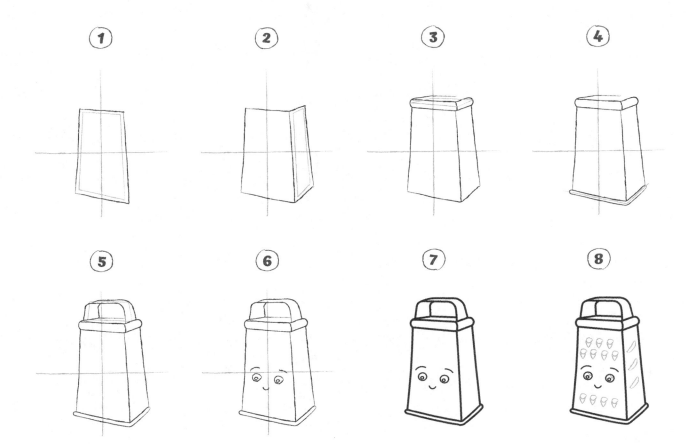

PRACTICE

WHISK & BOWL

PRACTICE

JAR OF JAM

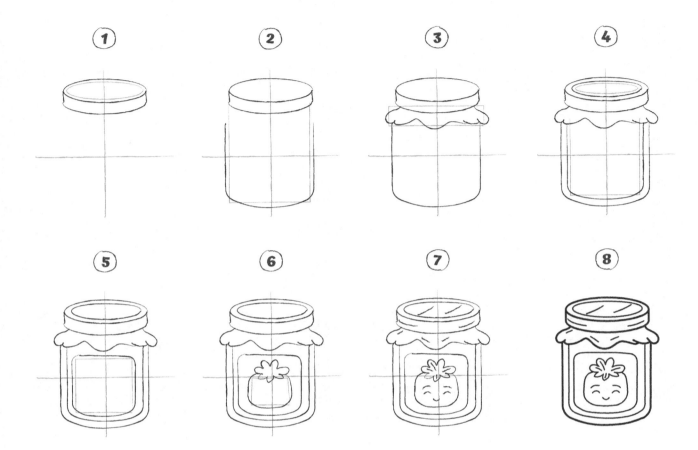

① ② ③ ④

⑤ ⑥ ⑦ ⑧

PRACTICE

SALT & PEPPER SHAKER

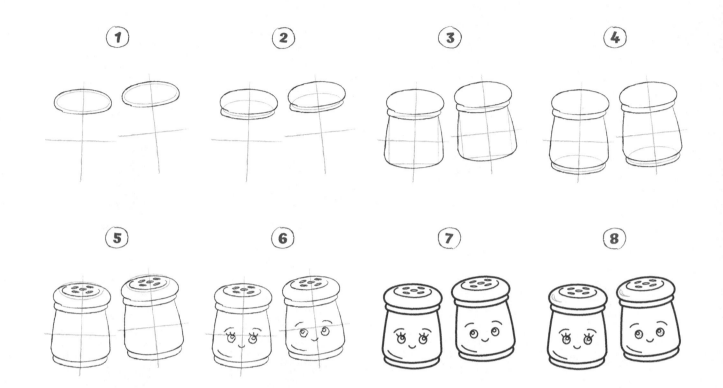

PRACTICE

TOASTER

PRACTICE

MICROWAVE

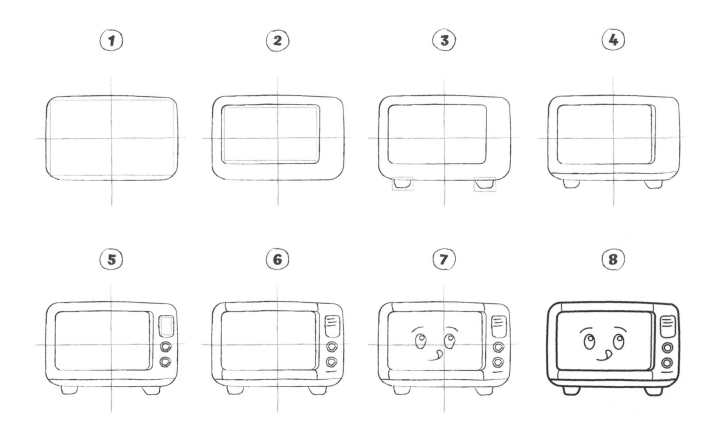

① ② ③ ④

⑤ ⑥ ⑦ ⑧

PRACTICE

BLENDER

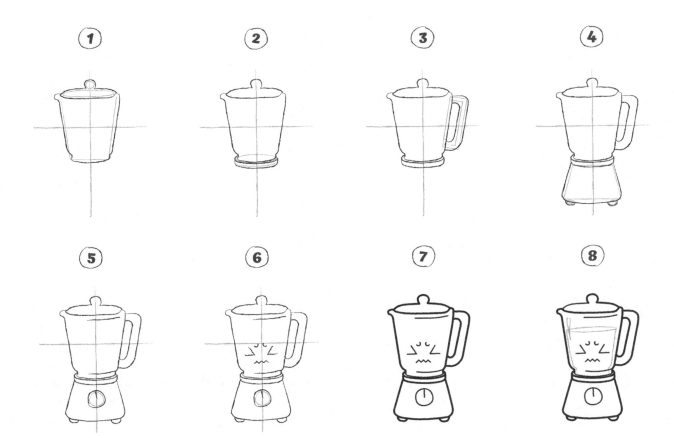

PRACTICE

COFFEE MAKER

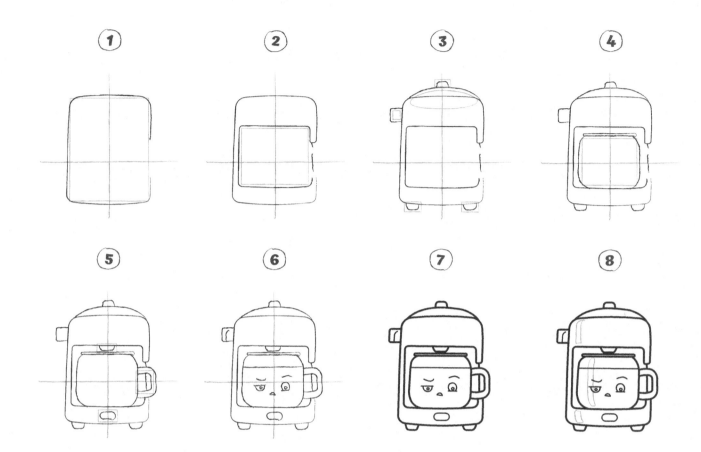

① ② ③ ④

⑤ ⑥ ⑦ ⑧

PRACTICE

ELECTRIC KETTLE

PRACTICE

MIXER

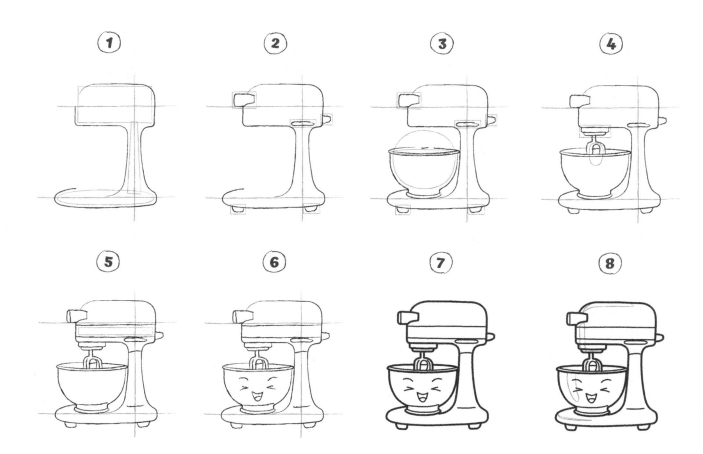

① ② ③ ④

⑤ ⑥ ⑦ ⑧

PRACTICE

FRIDGE

①

②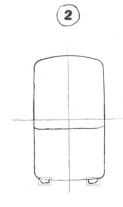

③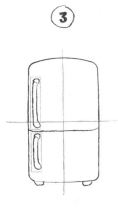

④

⑤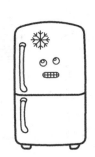

⑥

PRACTICE

WASHING MACHINE

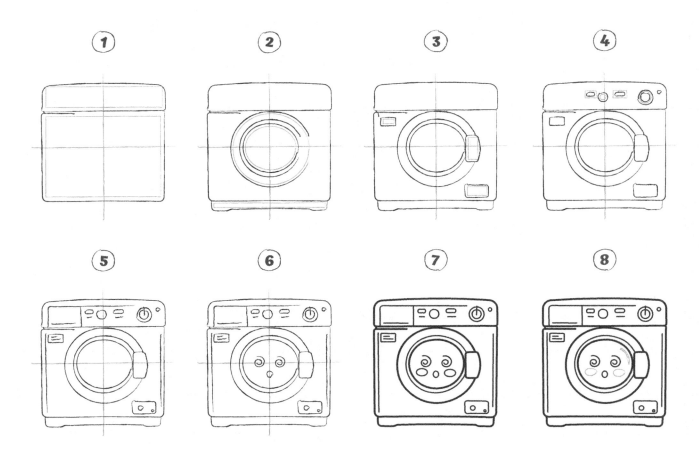

① ② ③ ④

⑤ ⑥ ⑦ ⑧

PRACTICE

IRON

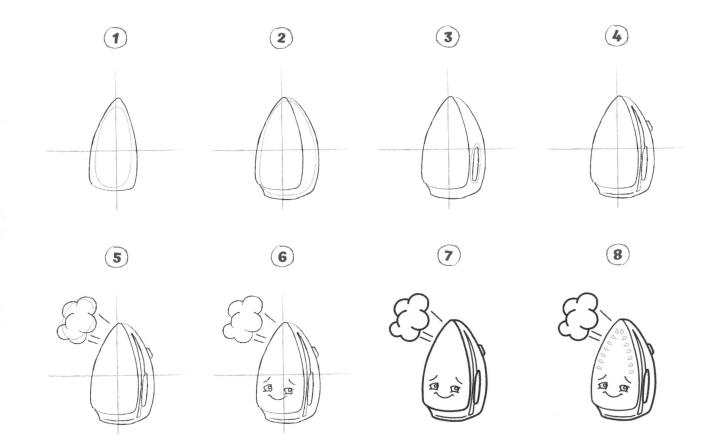

PRACTICE

HAIR DRYER

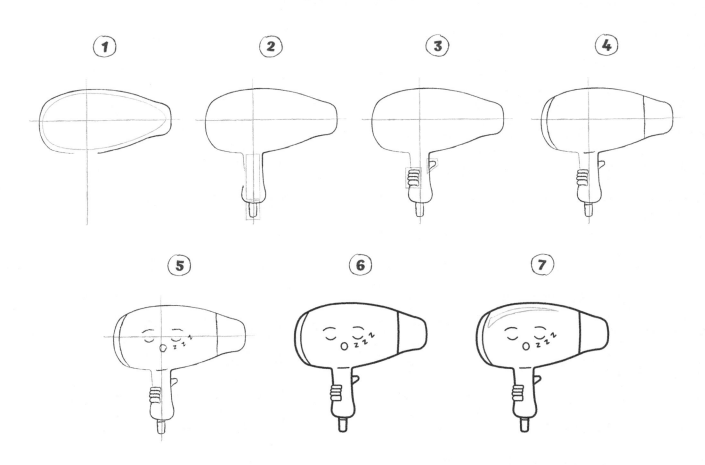

PRACTICE

GAME JOYSTICK

PRACTICE

PUZZLE

① ② ③

④ ⑤

PRACTICE

CHESS

PRACTICE

BALLOON

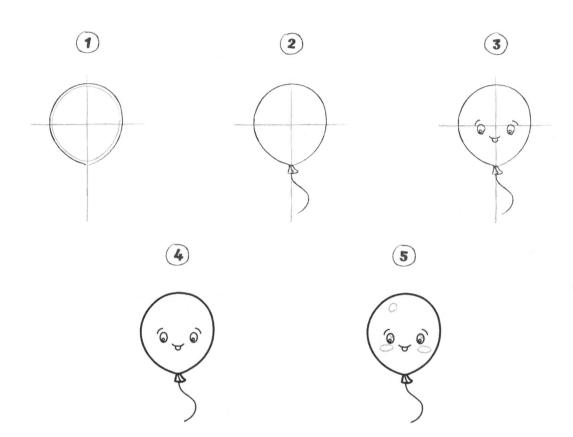

PRACTICE

BOWLING

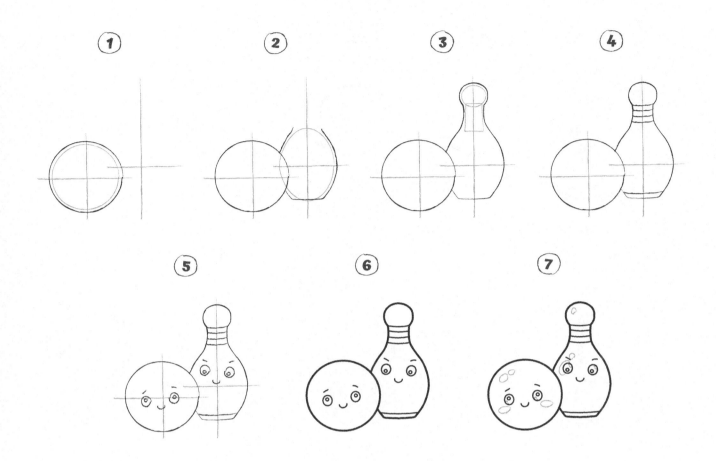

① ② ③ ④

⑤ ⑥ ⑦

PRACTICE

ROBOT

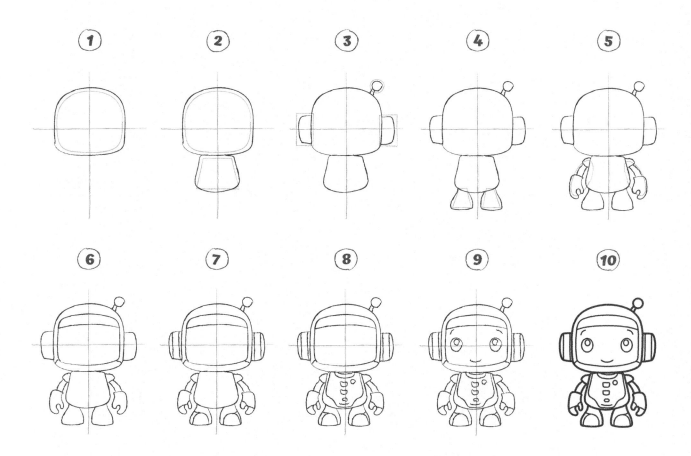

PRACTICE

SKATE

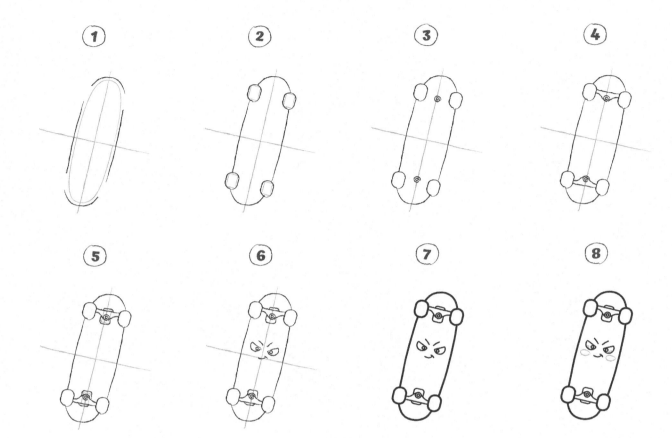

PRACTICE

BASEBALL

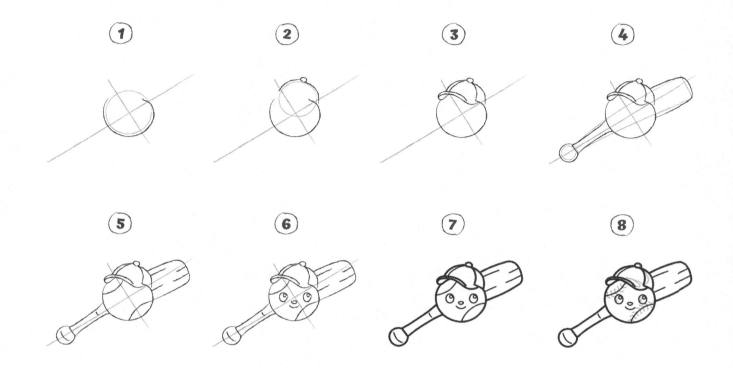

PRACTICE

FOOTBALL BALL

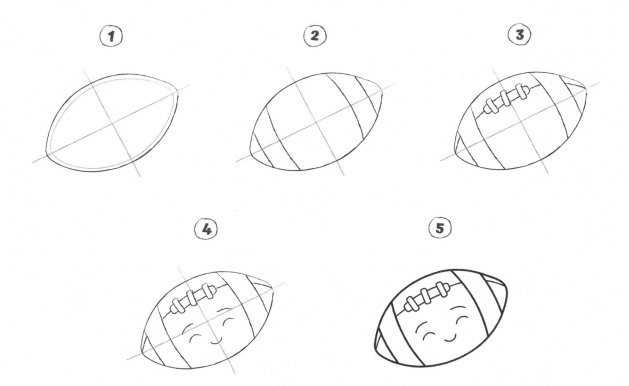

①   ②   ③

④   ⑤

PRACTICE

CHAMPION CUP

PRACTICE

ARTIST

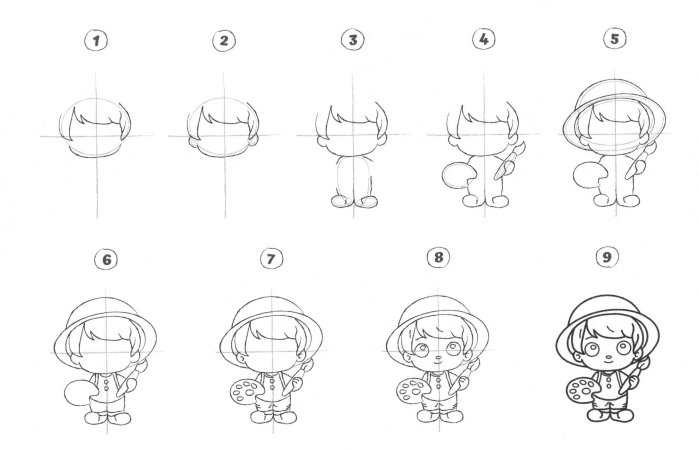

PRACTICE

STUDENT

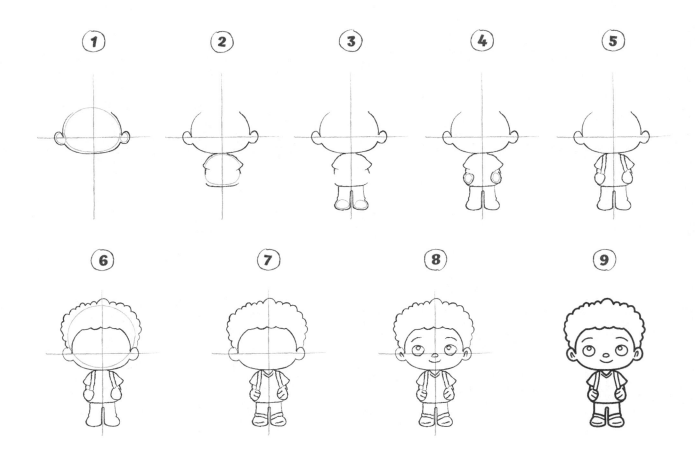

PRACTICE

TEACHER

PRACTICE

ROBBER

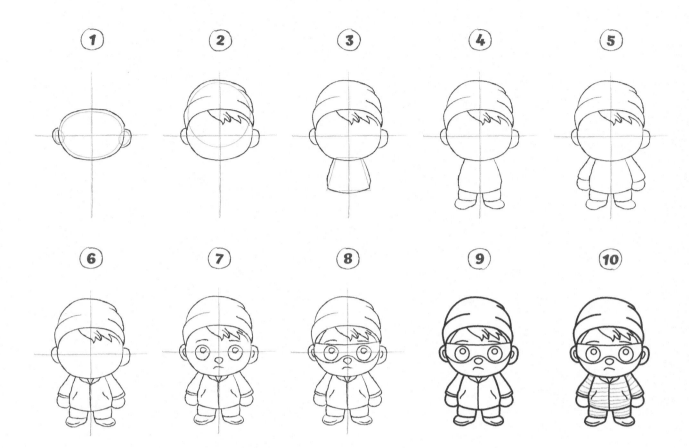

PRACTICE

POLICEMAN

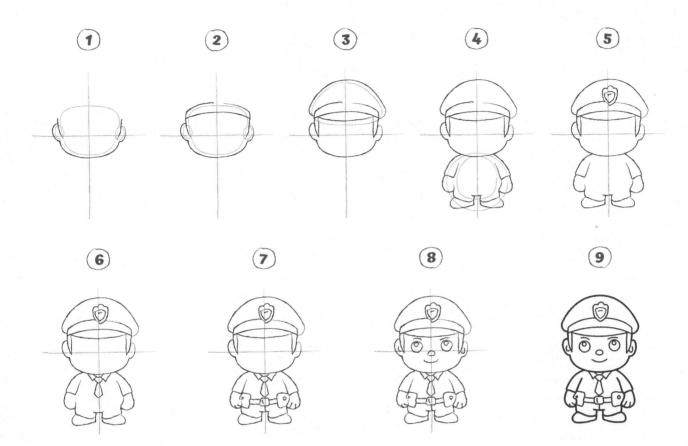

PRACTICE

RETIRED

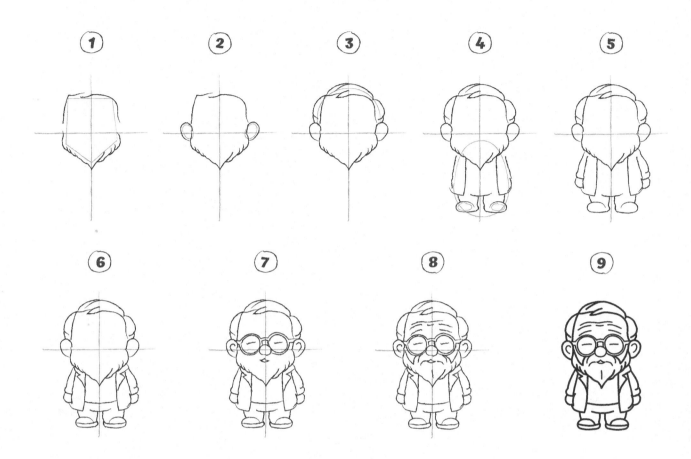

PRACTICE

DOCTOR

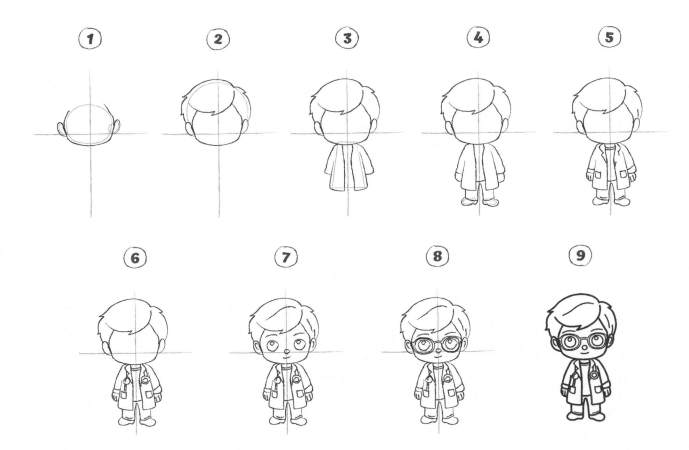

PRACTICE

FARMER

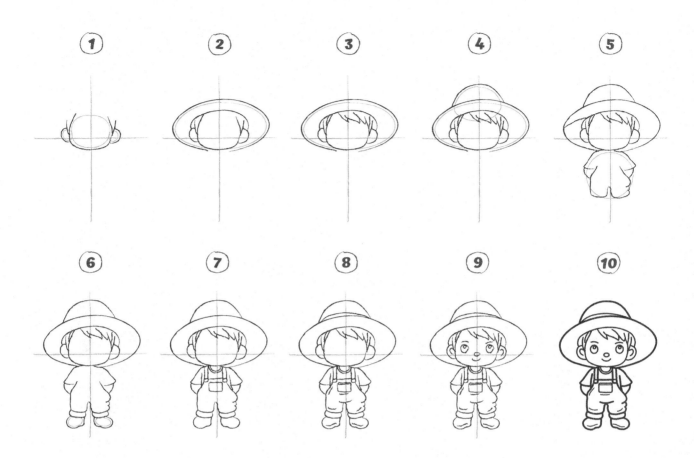

PRACTICE

BUSINESSMAN

① ② ③ ④

⑤ ⑥ ⑦ ⑧

PRACTICE

SPORTSMAN

PRACTICE

SCOOTER

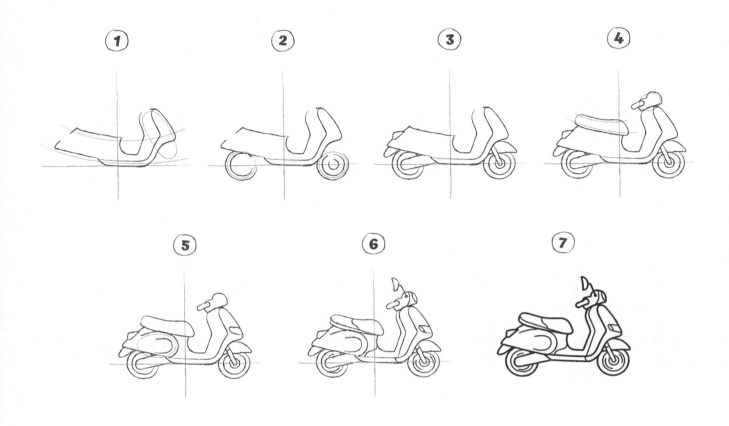

PRACTICE

CAR

PRACTICE

BICYCLE

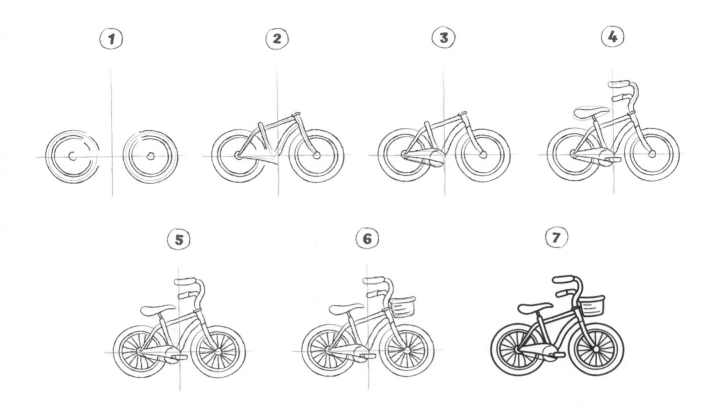

PRACTICE

MOTORCYCLE

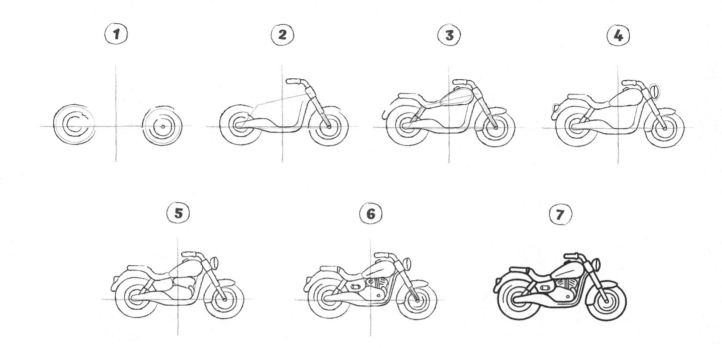

① ② ③ ④

⑤ ⑥ ⑦

PRACTICE

TRAIN

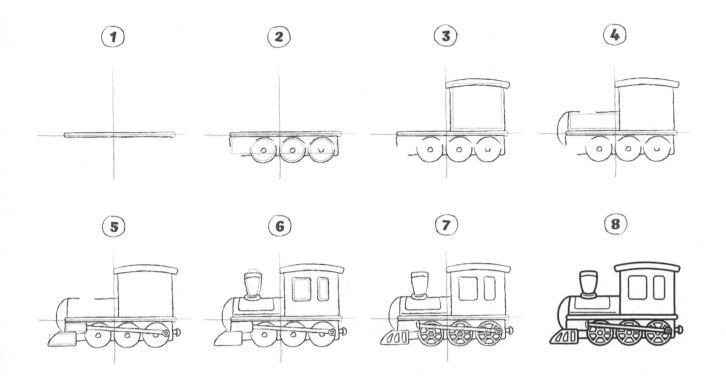

PRACTICE

AIRPLANE

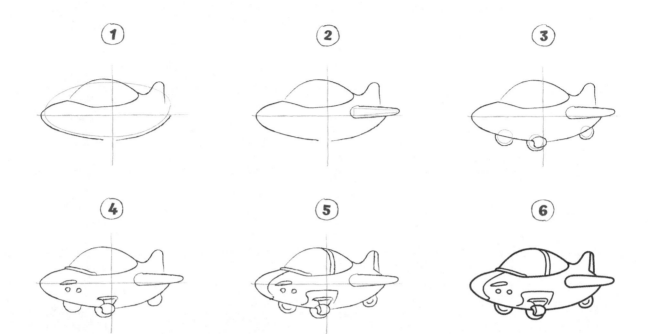

PRACTICE

AIRSHIP

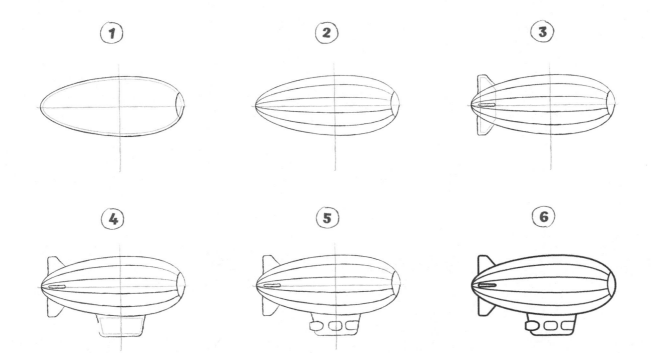

PRACTICE

HOT AIR BALLOON

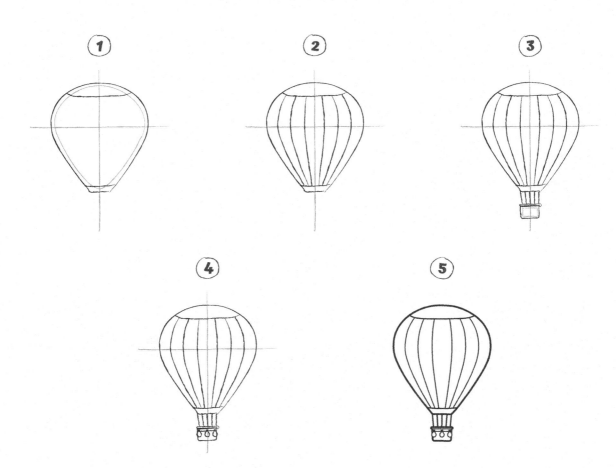

PRACTICE

SUBMARINE

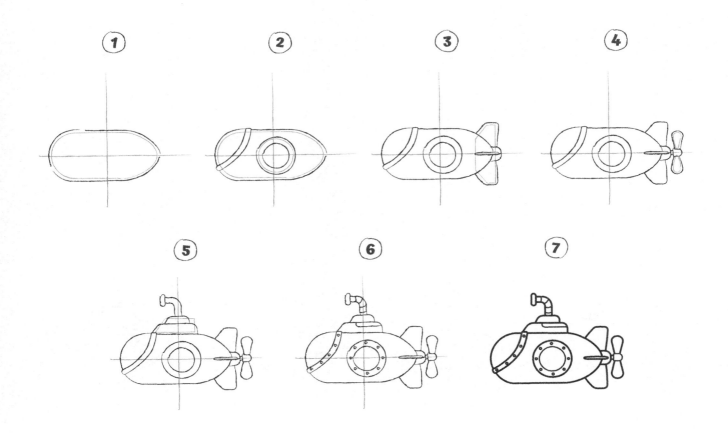

PRACTICE

SHIP

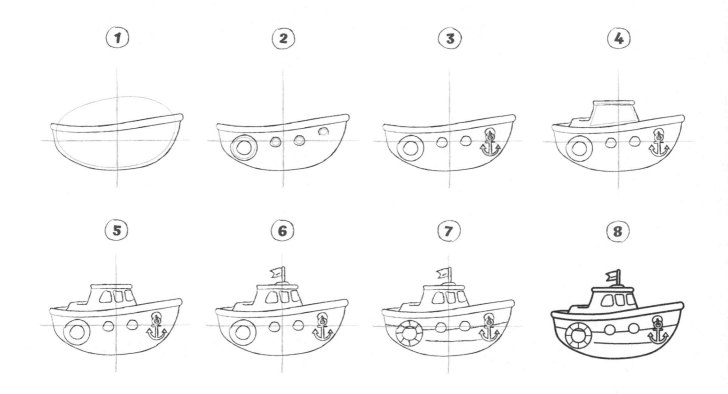

PRACTICE

SATURN

PRACTICE

ASTRONAUT

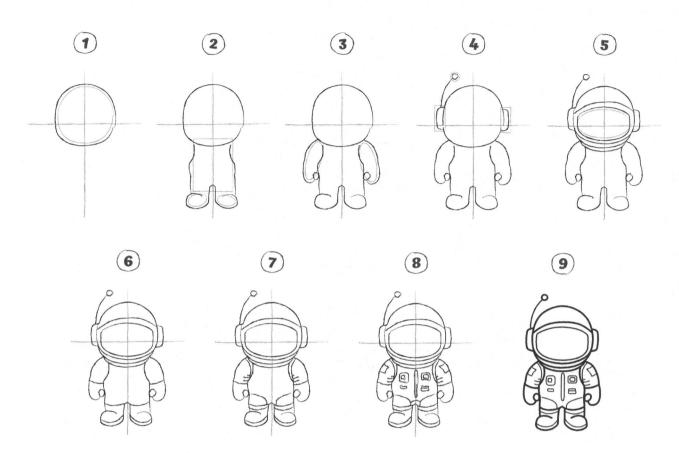

PRACTICE

TELESCOPE

PRACTICE

ROCKET

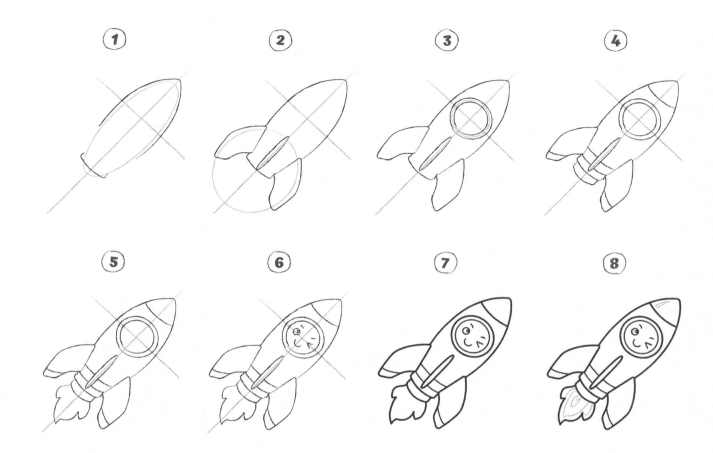

PRACTICE

ASTEROID

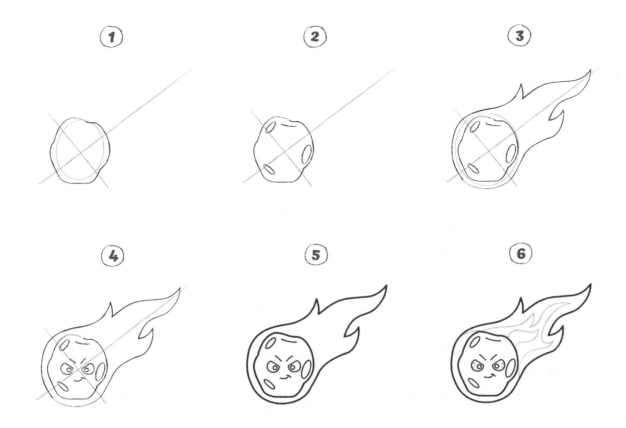

PRACTICE

ALIEN

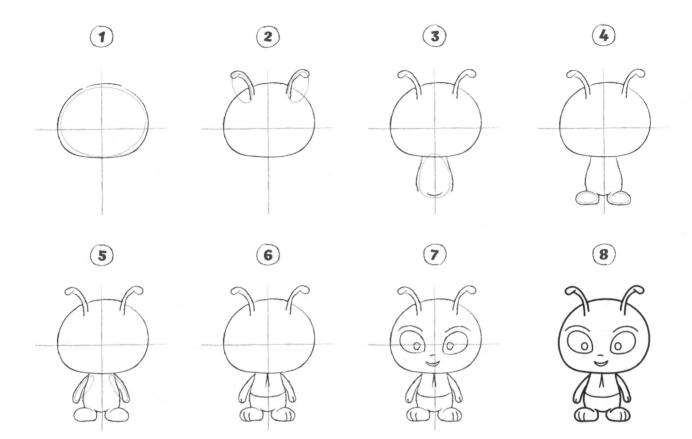

PRACTICE

UFO

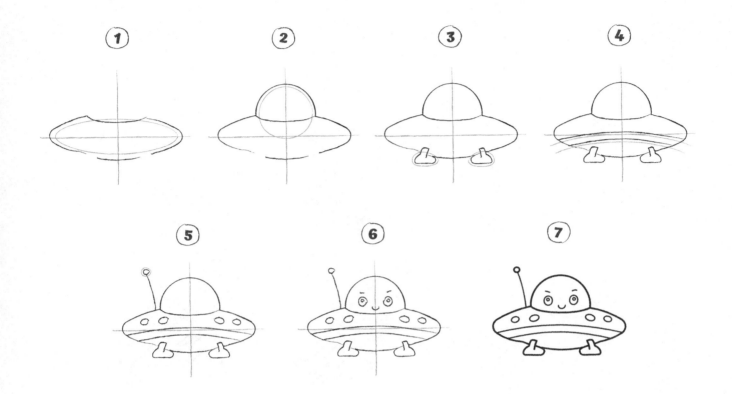

PRACTICE

SATELLITE

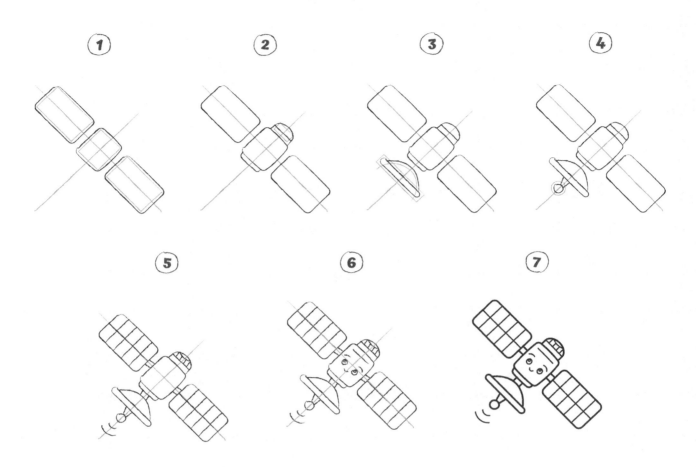

PRACTICE

ROVER

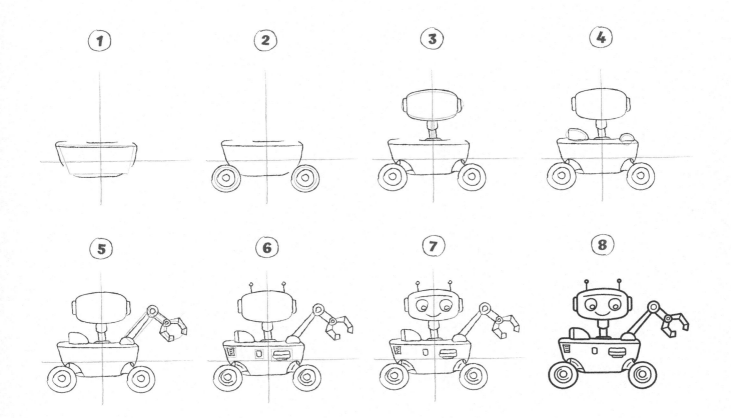

PRACTICE

EARTH

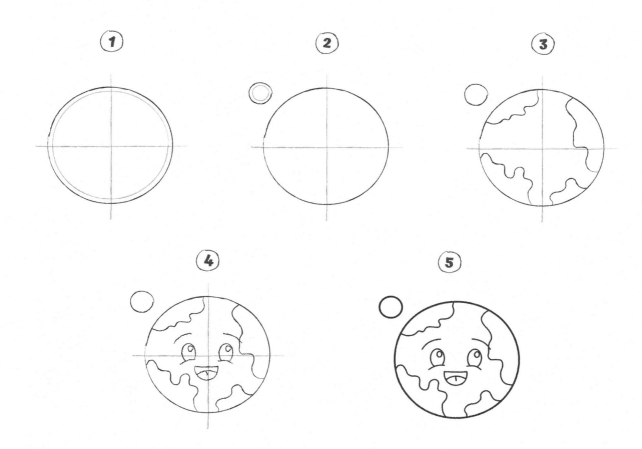

PRACTICE

GALAXY

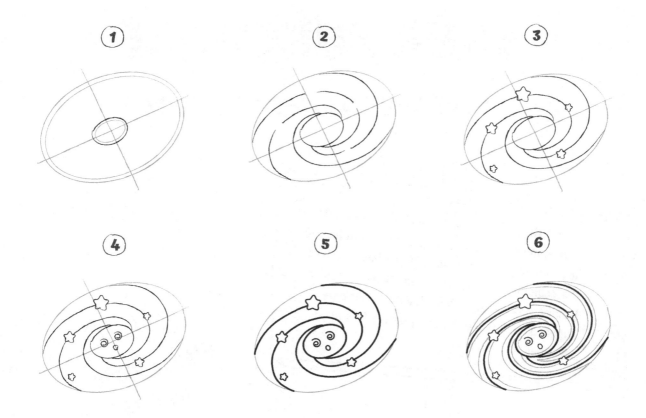

PRACTICE

THANK YOU FOR YOUR PURCHASE

HOPE YOU ENJOYED THIS BOOK

We are thrilled that you have chosen our book! Your opinion matters to us, and we would love to hear about your experience. If you have enjoyed the book and found it valuable, please consider leaving a fair review. Your feedback not only supports us but also helps other readers make informed decisions.

Please leave us a review!

Scan QR code

Thank you for taking the time to share your experience, we appreciate your support!

Made in the USA
Las Vegas, NV
11 June 2024